SCIENCE WORKS!

ENERGY

STEVE PARKER

For a free color catalog describing Gareth Stevens Publishing's list of high-quality books
and multimedia programs, call 1-800-542-2595 (USA) or 1-800-461-9120 (Canada).
Gareth Stevens Publishing's Fax: (414) 225-0377.
See our catalog, too, on the World Wide Web: http://gsinc.com

Library of Congress Cataloging-in-Publication Data

Parker, Steve.
    Energy / by Steve Parker; [illustrators . . . Steve Roberts, Clive Spong.]
      p. cm. — (Science works!)
    Includes index.
    Summary: Text and experiments demonstrate the nature
and uses of energy in its various forms.
    ISBN 0-8368-1962-4 (lib. bdg.)
    1. Force and energy—Juvenile literature. 2. Force and energy—
Experiments—Juvenile literature. 3. Power (Mechanics)—Juvenile
literature. 4. Power (Mechanics)—Experiments—Juvenile literature.
[1. Force and energy—Experiments. 2. Experiments.] I. Roberts,
Steve, ill. II. Spong, Clive, ill. III. Title. IV. Series: Parker, Steve.
Science works!
QC73.4.P37   1997
530—dc21   97-10475

First published in North America in 1997 by
Gareth Stevens Publishing
1555 North RiverCenter Drive, Suite 201
Milwaukee, Wisconsin 53212 USA

This U.S. edition © 1997 by Gareth Stevens, Inc. Created with original © 1995
Macdonald Young Books Ltd., Campus 400, Maylands Avenue, Hemel Hempstead,
Hertfordshire, England HP2 7EZ. Additional end matter © 1997 by Gareth Stevens, Inc.

Illustrators: Maltings Partnership, Steve Roberts, Clive Spong

Printed in Mexico

1 2 3 4 5 6 7 8 9 01 00 99 98 97

SCIENCE WORKS!

ENERGY

STEVE PARKER

Gareth Stevens Publishing
MILWAUKEE

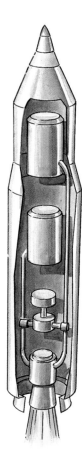

CONTENTS

Words that appear in the glossary are in **boldface** type the first time they occur in the text.

ENERGY

The word *energy* has separate meanings in different situations. If you have energy, you are busy and active. An energy-saving car uses less fuel than other cars. An energy-efficient washing machine uses less water, electricity, and laundry detergent than other washing machines. Energy is saved by recycling bottles and cans. Eating food gives you energy for living every day. In science, the word *energy* has a more restricted meaning. It is the ability to do work, or to make things happen.

In science, energy is not an object itself. It is a feature of some objects and of certain kinds of rays or waves. It comes in different forms, such as light, heat, sound, chemicals, movements, and radioactivity.

The story of energy

This book traces scientific ideas about energy from ancient times to the modern world of jet planes and nuclear power stations. Panels and boxes on almost every page present information in three different ways, as explained below.

The first section of the book shows that energy exists in many different forms. These can be changed from one form to another. But energy is never lost. The total amount always stays the same.

The second section describes movement as a familiar and important form of energy. Movements are produced by forces, and simple scientific rules show how force and motion are linked.

The third section shows how energy, forces, and movements are used in a variety of simple machines, from ramps and wedges to wheels and axles. Simple machines are combined to make more complicated machines, such as the change from a simple bicycle to a more complicated combine harvester.

The fourth section describes how energy is manipulated to make things move — by the use of engines. Fuels provide the energy for many different engines, from old-fashioned steam trains to the latest space rockets.

The last section shows that we are using energy at a tremendous rate. Coal, oil, gas, and other fossil fuels provide most of this energy, and they will soon be used up. We must plan ahead and save energy for the future.

FAMOUS FIRSTS

Knowledge thrives on firsts, such as the first person to discover a scientific law or make an invention. The *Famous Firsts* panels describe these first achievers.

DIY SCIENCE

Follow in the footsteps of well-known scientists by trying the tests and experiments in "Do-It-Yourself" form, using everyday materials, as shown in the *DIY Science* panels.

SPECIAL FX

Scientific processes and principles can have fascinating, even startling, results. The *Special FX* projects show you how to produce these special effects. Most items are readily available in your home.

TYPES OF ENERGY

It is impossible to imagine a world without energy. Almost everything that happens involves energy in one form or another. Without energy, nothing would move since motion represents energy. There would be no light because light is a form of energy. There would be no heat for the same reason. Sound is a type of energy, so this would be missing, too. Even matter itself — the **atoms** and **molecules** from which all things are made — is held together by forces that represent energy. Without energy, the world would be dark, still, silent, and cold.

A lightning bolt involves four forms of energy — the light of the flash, the electricity it contains, the intense heat, and the sound of the thunderclap.

SPECIAL FX

CHANGING ENERGY
Carry out a simple energy conversion by blowing up a balloon and letting it go.

You need *A balloon.*

1. Blow up a balloon in the normal way. You force air from your lungs into a confined space, blowing it into the balloon. Your chest muscles do this work.

2. Let go of the balloon. The stored energy represented by the pressurized air is turned into other forms. An obvious one is motion, as the balloon buzzes around. Are there others? Remember, sound is a form of energy.

Do you ever feel tired, worn out, and lacking in energy? If so, you probably want to just sit or lie still. Soon, however, you become rested and refreshed. You feel full of energy again. You want to get up, become active, and do things with a renewed spirit.

This is the way many people use the word *energy* in daily life. Its meaning in science is very similar and can be expressed fairly simply. Energy is the capacity to do work — to make

FAMOUS FIRSTS

The first time people used a form of energy, other than in their own bodies, was when they lit and controlled fires. The fire gave light to see by, and heat to keep warm and cook food. The first person to use the word *energy* in its modern scientific sense was English scientist Thomas Young (1773-1829) in the early 1800s. He referred to moving objects as having energy because they could do work, such as an ox pulling a plow.

*Almost half a million years ago, **Stone Age** people were controlling fire. They used its light and heat energy.*

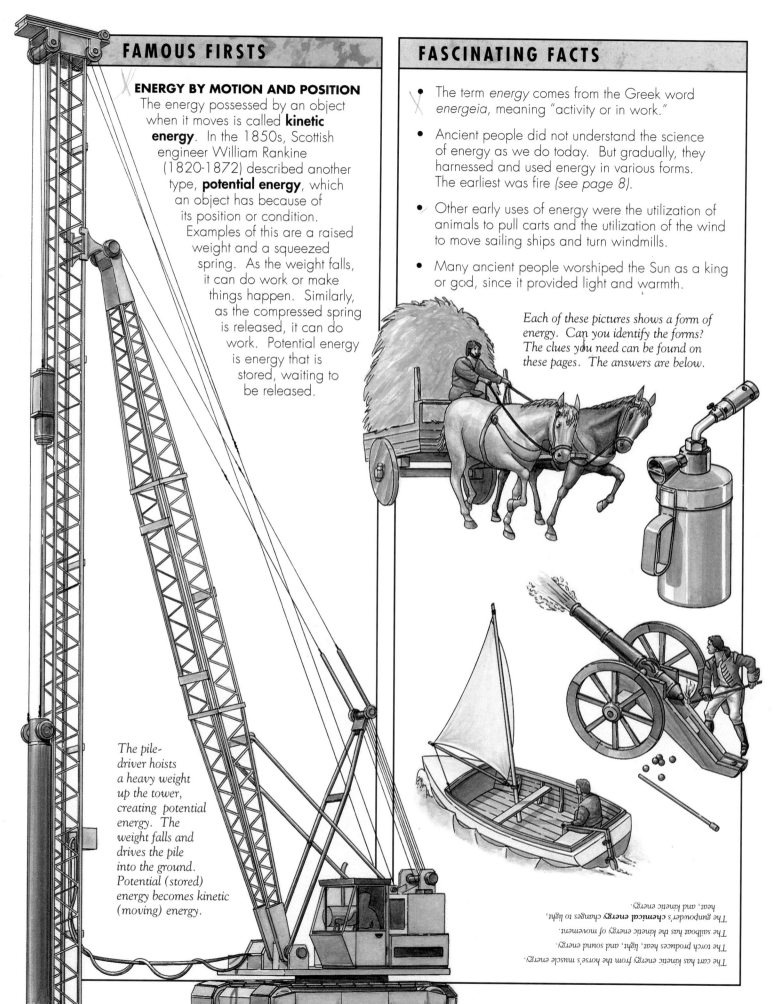

ENERGY BY MOTION AND POSITION

The energy possessed by an object when it moves is called **kinetic energy**. In the 1850s, Scottish engineer William Rankine (1820-1872) described another type, **potential energy**, which an object has because of its position or condition. Examples of this are a raised weight and a squeezed spring. As the weight falls, it can do work or make things happen. Similarly, as the compressed spring is released, it can do work. Potential energy is energy that is stored, waiting to be released.

The pile-driver hoists a heavy weight up the tower, creating potential energy. The weight falls and drives the pile into the ground. Potential (stored) energy becomes kinetic (moving) energy.

- The term *energy* comes from the Greek word *energeia*, meaning "activity or in work."

- Ancient people did not understand the science of energy as we do today. But gradually, they harnessed and used energy in various forms. The earliest was fire *(see page 8)*.

- Other early uses of energy were the utilization of animals to pull carts and the utilization of the wind to move sailing ships and turn windmills.

- Many ancient people worshiped the Sun as a king or god, since it provided light and warmth.

Each of these pictures shows a form of energy. Can you identify the forms? The clues you need can be found on these pages. The answers are below.

The cart has kinetic energy from the horse's muscle energy.
The torch produces heat, light, and sound energy.
The sailboat has the kinetic energy of movement.
The gunpowder's chemical energy changes to light, heat, and kinetic energy.

things happen and get things going. The situation rapidly becomes complicated, however, because energy can exist in so many different forms. Almost anything you can think of represents energy in one form or another.

Take a simple example — the bright Sun shining in the sky. How is energy involved? The Sun gives out light, which is one familiar and very important form of energy. Light makes things happen. Plants depend on the energy in sunlight for their very existence. Plants capture this energy by the chemical process of **photosynthesis** and use it to build their various parts and power their life processes. We depend on the energy in light to see. The light energy is changed in our eyes to the electrical energy of tiny nerve signals. These go to the brain and enable us to create a picture of our surroundings.

The Sun gives out other rays besides light rays. It produces ultraviolet rays. Humans cannot see ultraviolet light. But many types of animals, such as insects and frogs, can see it. Ultraviolet rays have the same basic nature as light rays. They are both electro-magnetic waves, and they are both a form of energy.

The Sun also gives out heat. This is another familiar and important form of energy. Heat makes things happen. It warms objects and changes them. The Sun's heat can change liquid water to invisible water vapor. This is why a puddle dries up in the Sun.

We can follow the energy trail farther. The Sun's heat warms certain parts of Earth more than others, due to the different heat-absorbing

FAMOUS FIRSTS

ENERGY EQUIVALENTS
English scientist James Joule (1818-1889) made great progress in the study of energy in the 1830s and 1840s. He saw how steam engines converted heat into movement. His precise, well-designed experiments showed how movement could be converted into heat. The same amount of movement always produced the same amount of heat. This led to the idea called the mechanical equivalent of heat. From this came the principle that very different types of energy — kinetic, potential, heat, sound, light, chemical, electrical, and so on — can all be measured in the same units.

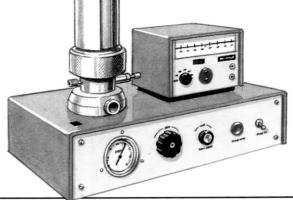

This scientific device is called a bomb calorimeter. It sets fire to, or explodes, a small sample of a substance such as food, wood, or coal. The heat released is measured extremely accurately, showing the amount of heat energy that was in the substance.

FASCINATING FACTS

- There are several units for measuring energy. One is the calorie. It was originally defined as a measure of heat, but it can be used to measure other forms of energy, such as the chemical energy in food. *(See the calorimeter above.)* Look on food packages for calorie counts.

- Another unit of energy is the watt-hour. It is mainly for measuring electrical energy, as used by an electric heater, for example.

- The modern standard unit that is used worldwide to measure energy or work is the joule, named after James Joule *(see above)*.

DIY SCIENCE

KEEPING WARM
On a cold day, you might rub your hands together to keep them warm. Try it now. This is another example of energy changing form. The energy-rich sugars in your blood came originally from your food. They supply your muscles with chemical energy. The muscles convert this to kinetic, or movement, energy. As the skin on your hands rubs together, the friction produces heat energy. Friction is very important in many energy changes *(see page 20)*.

THE ENERGY CAKE

The next time you do some baking, think about the energy involved and where it all comes from. This chart traces different forms of energy and how one type of energy is converted into another. You can see that, in all cases, the energy can be traced farther and farther back until it reaches the Sun. All living things, machines, and engines are powered by energy that came originally from the Sun. (There is one exception; see pages 44-45.)

You need

Two greased cake pans, mixing bowl, wooden spoon, metal tablespoon, 3/4 cup (150 grams) of butter, 3/4 cup (150 grams) of sugar, three eggs, 1 1/3 cups (150 grams) of flour, adult supervision.

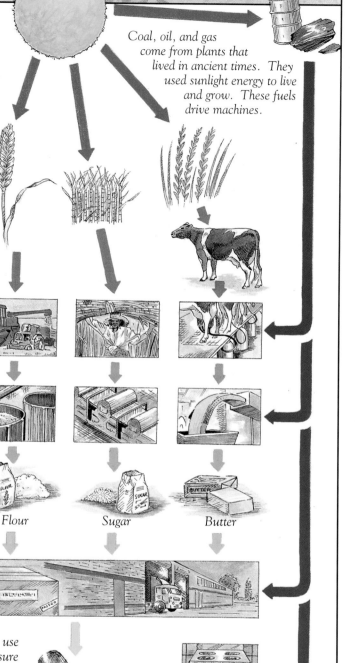

Coal, oil, and gas come from plants that lived in ancient times. They used sunlight energy to live and grow. These fuels drive machines.

Only a fraction of the Sun's energy reaches the surface of Earth. Grass, wheat, and sugar cane grow using sunlight energy. Cows eat grass, and chickens eat seeds for energy.

Eggs   Flour   Sugar   Butter

1. With the wooden spoon, mix the butter and sugar in the mixing bowl until light and fluffy.

2. Add the eggs one at a time, beating each one into the mixture with a tablespoon of flour.

3. Gently fold in the rest of the flour with the metal spoon. Spoon the final mixture into the two cake pans.

The body's muscles use energy as they measure and mix the ingredients. The oven uses gas or electricity that may be from a power station that uses fossil fuels.

4. Bake in an oven for 25 minutes at 350°F (180°C). Place on a rack to cool. Then put the cakes together with a filling in between.

Now that you have made the cake, eat a slice. Your body, like all living things, needs energy to live, grow, and maintain itself. A slice of cake provides enough energy for you to jog gently for half an hour. But think how much energy was used to make it. Would some fresh fruit be a more efficient way for your body to use the Sun's energy?

The finished cake.

11

An atomic bomb changes matter, in the form of parts of atoms, into incredible quantities of heat, light, and other energy.

MATTER AND ENERGY

The work of German-American scientist Albert Einstein (1879-1955) and others showed that energy and matter are not separate. Matter is the atoms and molecules that make up all substances. It can be changed into energy, so matter can be seen as a form of energy. This happens in an atomic or nuclear reaction. The first controlled nuclear reaction was in Chicago, Illinois, in 1942 *(see photo at left)*.

*In a **nuclear reaction**, the nuclei, the central parts of atoms, break down into slightly lighter particles. The difference in weight becomes massive quantities of heat energy.*

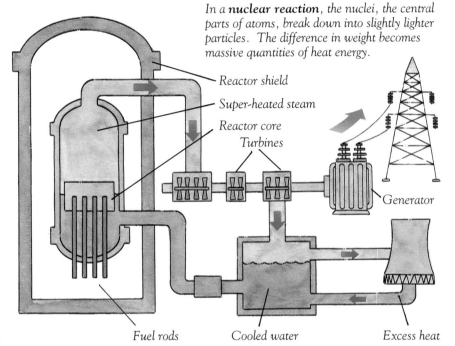

Reactor shield

Super-heated steam

Reactor core

Turbines

Generator

Fuel rods   Cooled water   Excess heat

nature of different surfaces, such as various colors of rocks, plants, soil, and water. This heat also passes to the air and warms it. As you can tell by watching smoke rise from a fire, warm air rises. So cooler air from elsewhere moves in to replace the rising warm air. This sideways flow of air is what we call wind. Wind is another form of energy because it involves movement or motion. We can use machines, such as windmills and wind turbines, to harness the energy of wind and make things happen — from pushing a sailboat to generating electricity.

This example shows several features of energy. First, as already mentioned, energy exists in many different forms. Secondly, energy can be changed or converted from one form to another. The Sun's warmth becomes the energy of moving air, or wind. This is converted, in turn, by a wind turbine into electrical energy.

Our world can be viewed as a vast, complicated, interconnected web of energy in its many forms.

DIY SCIENCE

CONSERVATION OF ENERGY

Following the work of James Joule *(see page 10)* and others, scientists realized that although energy can be converted from one form to another, it can never be created or destroyed. This is the principle of the conservation of energy.

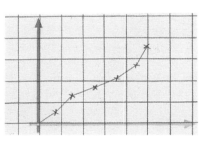

You need

Model car, piece of wood, books, protractor, pencil, ruler, paper.

Prop up the wood with some books to make a ramp. Measure its angle with the protractor. Release the car from the top, and measure how far it rolls along the floor. Repeat with the ramp at different angles. Draw a graph of ramp angles and rolling distances.

If the car is higher at the start, it has more potential energy. Following the principle of energy conservation, this changes to more kinetic energy, and it rolls farther. But friction (see page 20) limits the rolling distance.

FLYING ENERGY
This model airplane illustrates several of the principles connected with energy, such as conversion and conservation.

You need
Piece of balsa wood, glue, cardboard, tape, wire, rubber band, hook, plastic propeller (from a model shop).

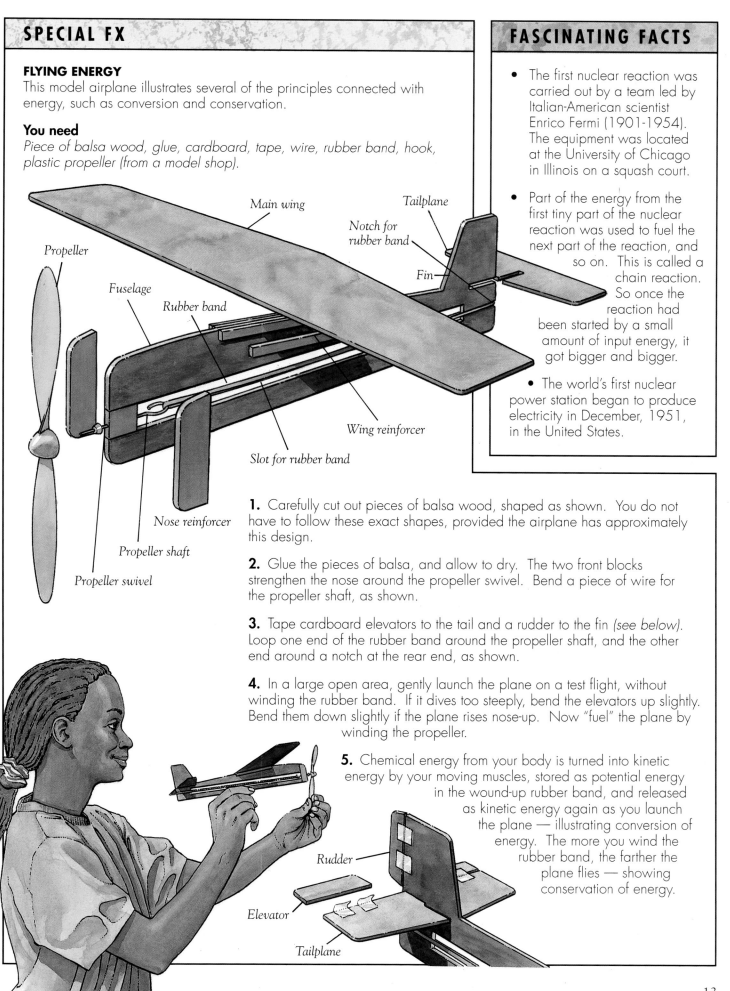

Propeller

Fuselage

Rubber band

Main wing

Tailplane

Notch for rubber band

Fin

Wing reinforcer

Slot for rubber band

Nose reinforcer

Propeller shaft

Propeller swivel

Rudder

Elevator

Tailplane

- The first nuclear reaction was carried out by a team led by Italian-American scientist Enrico Fermi (1901-1954). The equipment was located at the University of Chicago in Illinois on a squash court.

- Part of the energy from the first tiny part of the nuclear reaction was used to fuel the next part of the reaction, and so on. This is called a chain reaction. So once the reaction had been started by a small amount of input energy, it got bigger and bigger.

- The world's first nuclear power station began to produce electricity in December, 1951, in the United States.

1. Carefully cut out pieces of balsa wood, shaped as shown. You do not have to follow these exact shapes, provided the airplane has approximately this design.

2. Glue the pieces of balsa, and allow to dry. The two front blocks strengthen the nose around the propeller swivel. Bend a piece of wire for the propeller shaft, as shown.

3. Tape cardboard elevators to the tail and a rudder to the fin *(see below)*. Loop one end of the rubber band around the propeller shaft, and the other end around a notch at the rear end, as shown.

4. In a large open area, gently launch the plane on a test flight, without winding the rubber band. If it dives too steeply, bend the elevators up slightly. Bend them down slightly if the plane rises nose-up. Now "fuel" the plane by winding the propeller.

5. Chemical energy from your body is turned into kinetic energy by your moving muscles, stored as potential energy in the wound-up rubber band, and released as kinetic energy again as you launch the plane — illustrating conversion of energy. The more you wind the rubber band, the farther the plane flies — showing conservation of energy.

FORCES AND MOVEMENT

Everything is moving. Even as you sit still in a chair, your body is moving. Your lungs are breathing, and your heart is beating. In addition, the chair and the room are on the surface of Earth, which spins around once each day. And Earth is flying through space on its yearly orbit around the Sun. The pushings and pullings that make things move are called forces.

Moving objects possess a type of energy, called kinetic energy. But what is it that makes things move in the first place? The answer is forces. Like energy, there are many different kinds of forces. To understand the modern view of forces and movements, it helps to look back thousands of years to the early scientific thinkers.

Aristotle (384-322 B.C.) recorded his ideas about motion. Like many scientists of his time, he believed that everything on Earth is made of four basic elements — earth, air, fire, and water. These were mixed in different amounts to produce clouds, rocks, trees, animals, humans, and other objects.

Such earthbound objects moved only if a force pushed or pulled them. This is still roughly the view today. But for Aristotle and other ancients, the heavens →

Amusement park rides put people through amazing movements and forces. Scientific calculations are carried out to make sure the people and the equipment can take the strain safely.

FAMOUS FIRSTS

A NEW APPROACH

Italian scientist Galileo Galilei (1564-1642) broke with tradition. He was not prepared to simply accept the traditional ancient teachings. He was among the first scientists to do his own tests and experiments. This was a startling idea for the time. Very few people did experiments. Galileo measured how long it took for objects of different weights to fall the same distance. He showed that light objects fell just as fast as heavy ones, contrary to the accepted view. He also supported the controversial idea that Earth was not the center of all things. He believed Earth traveled around the Sun.

It is said that to observe falling objects, Galileo dropped stones and cannonballs from the Tower of Pisa in Italy. In those days, the tower was just beginning to lean.

Long ago, people made models, called orrerys, showing how the Earth, Moon, and Sun moved. This orrery shows the Sun at the center with other bodies revolving around it.

- **Pendulums** are used to measure gravity. As the experiment below shows, the time of a pendulum's back-and-forth swing, which is called an **oscillation**, is affected by two main factors. These are the length of the pendulum and the force of gravity. Very accurate pendulums tested in different parts of the world show that the force of gravity is not the same everywhere. This is because Earth is not a perfect sphere. Equatorial regions are slightly farther from Earth's center, and so the force of gravity there is slightly less.

SPECIAL FX

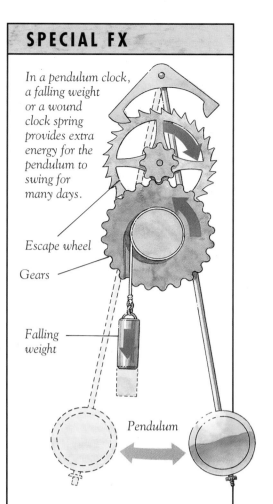

In a pendulum clock, a falling weight or a wound clock spring provides extra energy for the pendulum to swing for many days.

Escape wheel

Gears

Falling weight

Pendulum

DIY SCIENCE

THE PENDULUM

A pendulum always takes the same time for one complete swing, no matter how far it moves.

You need

Small bag of marbles for the pendulum bob, string, firm hook or other attachment, stopwatch.

1. Set up a pendulum, as shown, with the longest string possible. Make it swing a short way. Time ten complete back-and-forth swings.

2. Make the pendulum swing much farther. Time ten swings again. Do they take the same time?

3. Make the pendulum heavier by adding marbles. Repeat steps 1 and 2. Which factors affect the timing of each swing?

THE PENDULUM CLOCK

After timing your pendulum with a stopwatch *(see left)*, you could use its regular swings or oscillations as the "ticks" of a clock. Galileo had the same idea of using a pendulum as a clock. The year before he died, he produced the very first design for a pendulum clock. The first practical version was built by Dutch scientist Christiaan Huygens about sixteen years later.

A mathematical formula, or sum, links the length of a pendulum with the force of gravity and the time for each oscillation (back-and-forth swing). For example, a pendulum 9.8 inches (24.82 centimeters) long has an oscillation of exactly one second.

were different.) They believed the Sun, Moon, stars, and other heavenly bodies were made of a fifth element — ether. These bodies moved because they were locked in transparent layers that circled Earth. Their movement was majestically circular. It was the perfect motion of objects fashioned by gods and spirits.

The idea that there is a difference between heavenly motion, with its circular paths, and the many and varied movements here on Earth continued in one form or another for almost two thousand years. This belief was held by the Catholic church to show God's grand plan. It was commonly believed that movements on Earth were imperfect and impure due to human failings. But outside Earth, everything moved and revolved in a perfect way, with Earth at the center of it all.

FAMOUS FIRSTS

NEWTON'S LAWS OF MOTION

Sir Isaac Newton was the first person to identify the basic laws of motion. The laws may seem simple today, but at the time, they were a tremendous advance. They gave scientists a new basis for ideas and calculations. They are:

First law An object will continue to stay still or move in the same direction and at the same speed, unless it is acted on by an outside force.

Second law The change in direction and speed of an object is linked to the direction and the amount of the force.

Third law For every action there is an equal and opposite reaction. This action and reaction is connected to the idea of **momentum** *(see page 22).*

One ball hits another ball. This is the action. The first ball goes off at one angle and the second ball moves off at another angle. This is the reaction, according to the third law. Their combined momentums (see page 22) are equivalent to the momentum of the first ball before the collision.

DIY SCIENCE

NEWTON PLAYS POOL

A pool table is ideal for testing Newton's laws of motion. The balls bounce off each other well, and they roll easily on a very smooth surface. However, the problem of friction always affects experiments such as these. As a ball rolls along, it bumps into the molecules of gases that make up air. The molecules are incredibly tiny. But the millions of collisions gradually slow the ball down, according to Newton's third law. This slowing-down effect is called air resistance.

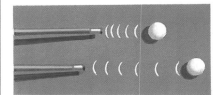

When you hit a ball while playing pool, you apply an outside force to get it moving. The ball then rolls in a straight line at an approximately constant speed, according to Newton's first law because hardly any forces act on it. When hit with a bigger force, it goes faster.

The ball hits the cushion. This applies a force at an angle to the ball's movement. So the ball changes direction, according to the second law.

SPECIAL FX

A SPINNING BALL

If you play Ping-Pong or tennis, you may know about topspin and backspin. They can be explained using Newton's laws of motion. Hit a ball at an angle, and it spins through the air. This produces lower air pressure on one side, compared with the other. This reduces the air resistance on that side. With unequal forces on its sides, the ball travels in a curved path.

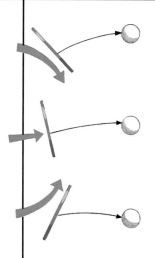

For backspin, hit the ball with the paddle angled upward. The bottom of the ball spins forward.

For no spin, the paddle meets the ball directly at right angles.

For topspin, hit and slice the ball with the paddle angled downward. The top of the ball spins forward.

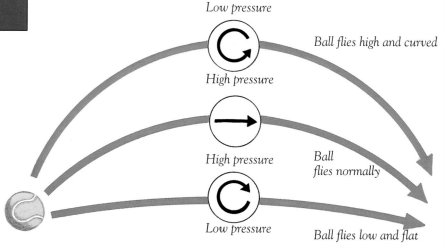

Low pressure

Ball flies high and curved

High pressure

High pressure

Ball flies normally

Low pressure

Ball flies low and flat

The spinning ball makes air move faster on the side spinning forward. This creates lower air pressure, and there is less force on this side.

DIY SCIENCE

THE MOTION MACHINE

This demonstration toy, called Newton's cradle, shows the laws of motion — especially the third one.

You need
Wooden balls or large beads with holes through them (the harder and heavier, the better), thin string, a file (for filing wood), two pencils, four cardboard tubes (from paper toweling).

1. Carefully file six notches in each pencil, as shown. Space the notches as far apart as the size of a ball, so that when the cradle is assembled, the balls just touch each other. File a notch in one end of each cardboard tube.

2. Thread string through each ball. Secure them by either tying a knot or using a smaller bead *(see left)*. Arrange the tubes, pencils, and balls as pictured *at right*.

3. Lift one ball, keeping the string taut, and let it swing down. As it hits its neighbor, the force is transmitted along the row of balls to the one at the other end. It shows an equal and opposite reaction by swinging out. Try swinging more balls for equal reactions at the other end.

FASCINATING FACTS

- Sir Isaac Newton was a man of many discoveries, such as the discovery of the nature of the light **spectrum**. But he also argued over scientific issues for many years with German mathematician Gottfried Leibniz and English physicist Robert Hooke.

Then scientists such as Nicolaus Copernicus, Johannes Kepler, and Galileo Galilei observed the night sky with the newly invented telescope. They showed that the movements of heavenly bodies would be much simpler if Earth revolved around the Sun, rather than the reverse. In the early seventeenth century, Galileo became involved in a battle between the authority of the Church and the truth of its teachings, and the freedom of scientists to carry out experiments and express new views.

Galileo himself carried out many studies of forces and movements. He watched and measured swinging pendulums and flying cannonballs. He showed that many ancient ideas, such as the belief that heavier objects fall faster than light ones of the same size, were not true. These results and Galileo's attitude helped scientists obtain more freedom to carry out tests and to propose new theories. As a result, science entered an era of renewed progress.

The next great figure to consider forces and movements was Sir Isaac Newton. He was born in 1642 — the year Galileo died. With his brilliant reasoning and the tool of mathematics, Newton devised three basic laws of motion. He even invented a new branch of mathematics called differential calculus. With it, the movements of objects that are speeding up or slowing down, whose speeds are

FAMOUS FIRSTS

AROUND THE SUN
For centuries, people believed the Sun, Moon, and the planets moved in perfect circles, with Earth at the center. German scientist Johannes Kepler (1571-1630) believed in the ideas of Copernicus — that Earth and the other planets orbited the Sun. He discovered that these heavenly bodies did not travel in circles — they moved in oval orbits called **ellipses**. Kepler devised laws of planetary motion to predict the path of each planet.

Kepler's first law says that the planets trace a shape called an ellipse as they orbit the Sun. The Sun is not central, but slightly to one side, at a point called the focus of the ellipse.

Earth

Equal areas

Kepler's second law says that an imaginary line joining a planet to the Sun traces equal areas in equal times. This means the planets speed up when they are nearer the Sun.

DIY SCIENCE

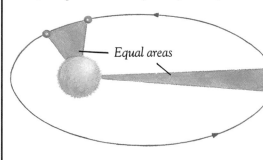

LEANING INTO THE CORNER
Moving in curves or circles means a combination of forward and sideways forces, as this test shows.

You need
A bicycle

Body weight

Sideways force

Forward motion

1. While riding a bicycle, try turning a corner without leaning to one side. It cannot be done.

2. Try again, leaning "into the corner." This shifts some of your weight to one side, and produces a sideways force. According to Newton's second law, you are moved by this force, in the direction in which it acts — sideways — in addition to your forward motion.

To obtain the best forces when cornering, racing motorcyclists lean so far that their knees touch the ground.

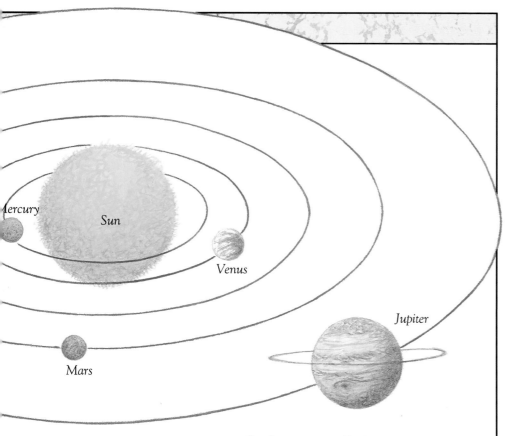

The planets are usually shown going around the Sun in perfect circles. But in fact, their orbits are oval-shaped ellipses, and some overlap.

- From the time of ancient Greek astronomer Ptolemy (A.D. 90-170), people believed in the geocentric system. This placed Earth at the center, with the Sun, planets, and stars going around it. This was the accepted view for about fourteen centuries.

- Polish astronomer Nicolaus Copernicus (1473-1543) proposed the heliocentric system. The Sun was at the center, with the planets going around it. The heliocentric system was a simpler explanation. After the work of Kepler and Galileo, it became the accepted view.

SPECIAL FX

THE GYROSCOPE
Have you ever studied the motion of a **gyroscope**? It is not just a scientific toy. Gyroscopes have many important uses in real life, especially for stability and navigation in ships, submarines, planes, and rockets. As a gyroscope wheel spins, it has a large momentum (see page 22) in a circle, called angular momentum. An object with straight or linear momentum tries to keep moving in a straight line. A gyroscope tends to continue spinning. It resists outside forces because of its angular momentum. A system of pivots allows the wheel to remain in the same position even as the outer frame changes position. A spinning top is a gyroscope without the outer frame.

The gyroscope tends to stay in the same position, so it can balance on a "tightrope" or even a single point.

SPECIAL FX

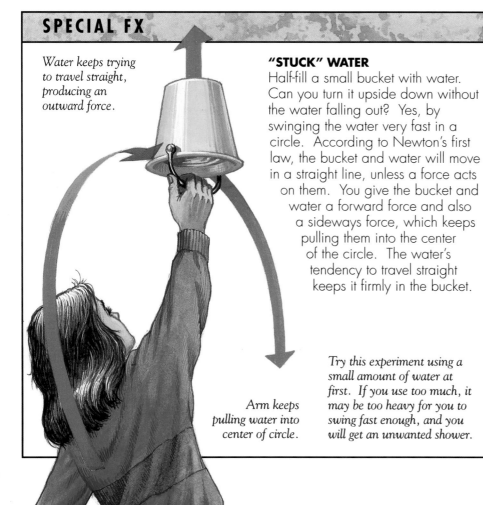

Water keeps trying to travel straight, producing an outward force.

"STUCK" WATER
Half-fill a small bucket with water. Can you turn it upside down without the water falling out? Yes, by swinging the water very fast in a circle. According to Newton's first law, the bucket and water will move in a straight line, unless a force acts on them. You give the bucket and water a forward force and also a sideways force, which keeps pulling them into the center of the circle. The water's tendency to travel straight keeps it firmly in the bucket.

Try this experiment using a small amount of water at first. If you use too much, it may be too heavy for you to swing fast enough, and you will get an unwanted shower.

Arm keeps pulling water into center of circle.

constantly changing, could be calculated.

Newton also came up with the idea of the force of **gravity**. Whether this really happened after an apple fell on his head is uncertain. Gravity is an attracting or pulling force exerted by all objects, no matter how small. Even the head of a pin has gravitational attraction. However, this is so small that it is never really noticed in daily life.

The gravitational force of much bigger objects, such as mountains, is more noticeable. It can affect the sensitive navigation equipment of airplanes. The gravitational force of an even more gigantic object dominates our lives. This is the gravity of Earth itself. It pulls objects towards its center. Earth's gravity gives objects potential energy (*see page 9*) because of their position. It gives objects kinetic energy as they move, commonly known as falling to the ground.

The gravitational pull of another massive object, the Moon, produces the ocean's tides on Earth. And the gravitational attraction of the biggest object in our solar system, the Sun, keeps Earth and the other eight planets traveling around it, year after year.

Newton published his main ideas in a book, usually known as *The Principia*, in 1687. It was one of the most important scientific works ever. *The Principia* formed the framework for the physical sciences, such as mechanics and astronomy, for the following two centuries.

There are two more ideas connected with forces and movements. One is **inertia**. This is the tendency of an object to keep doing what it has been doing — either

THE PROBLEM OF FRICTION

When two surfaces move against each other, they rub, scrape, and resist the movement. This is **friction** — a force that resists motion between two surfaces in contact. It usually turns kinetic energy (the energy of movement) into heat energy, so the rubbing parts become warm. Friction is a problem in many machines. Wanted movement turns into unwanted heat. The very first wheels and axles (*see page 32*) underwent great friction and wear. Since then, engineers have developed parts called bearings that reduce friction.

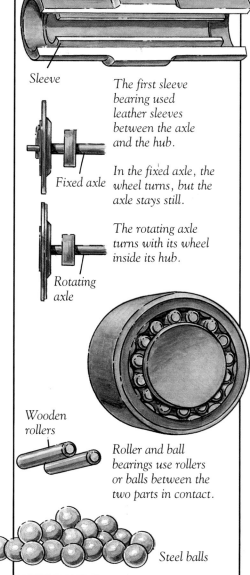

Sleeve

The first sleeve bearing used leather sleeves between the axle and the hub.

Fixed axle

In the fixed axle, the wheel turns, but the axle stays still.

Rotating axle

The rotating axle turns with its wheel inside its hub.

Wooden rollers

Roller and ball bearings use rollers or balls between the two parts in contact.

Steel balls

GETTING RID OF FRICTION

Build a car without worrying about friction, and it will be useless. Then improve the design by getting rid of as much friction as possible.

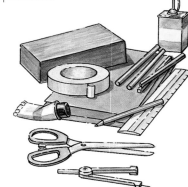

You need

Thick cardboard, block of wood, scissors, tape, wood squares, dowels, glue, pencil, compasses, lubricating oil.

1. Carefully cut the cardboard to make a high, upright cab for the car, as pictured. Using square pieces of wood as axles, cut axle brackets from cardboard, and tape or glue them to the body.

- Water and air are both fluids — they can flow. But water is much "thicker" than air. More friction is met when an object moves through it. In other words, water resistance is much greater than air resistance. You would discover this if you were to try to run in waist-high water in a swimming pool. This is why sharks, whales, dolphins, and swordfish are very smooth and streamlined.

- Sperm whales were once hunted for their body oil, a quality lubricant.

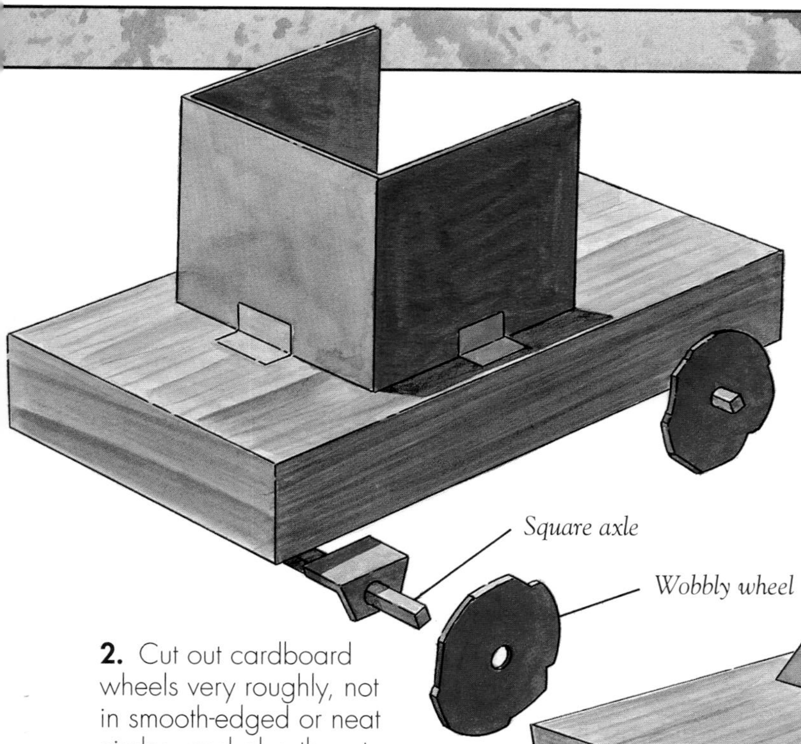

3. Now for the second version, the "Friction-Free Special." Reduce the car's friction due to air resistance (see page 16) by making the cab lower, sloped-back, and streamlined. Use dowels for the axles, which spin more easily. Add a drop of lubricating oil at the axle-bracket bearing to further reduce friction.

4. Cut out perfectly circular, smooth-edged cardboard wheels. Glue the axles into the exact center. This reduces the type of friction called rolling resistance. Which version of the car is best?

Square axle

Wobbly wheel

2. Cut out cardboard wheels very roughly, not in smooth-edged or neat circles, and glue them to the axles. Try rolling this version of the car, called the "Friction Special." How far does it go? Can it move at all?

SPECIAL FX

FIRE WITH FRICTION

The rubbing and scraping associated with friction can produce enough heat to start a fire. People long ago started fires by rubbing dry sticks together until the heat was enough to make the sticks smolder and light. Another method is to strike certain kinds of rocks, such as flints, together. The force of the sudden impact and friction produce a spark, which can set dry twigs and leaves on fire. Today, these skills have been largely lost. Other methods, such as striking a match, are used.

Homo erectus or "upright human" probably struck rocks together to start a fire half a million years ago.

moving or standing still — until a force acts on it and changes things. A cannonball's inertia keeps it flying through the air. If no forces at all act on the cannonball, it would keep going in a straight line forever. But the forces of air resistance (*see page 16*) and gravity slow it down and make it fall to the ground.

The second idea is that of **momentum**. The momentum of a moving object is similar to (but not the same as) its kinetic energy. It rises with the speed of an object and with its mass — what is usually called weight. A speeding locomotive has far more momentum than a rolling pea. But a pea traveling at an incredibly high speed could have the same momentum as a locomotive rolling very slowly.

By the 1900s, scientists were discovering more about outer space, with its planets and moons, and the world of inner space, with its atoms and smaller particles. It was clear that Newton's laws of motion and gravity were not the complete answer. Newton's laws described the Universe, and all of the objects and movements in it, as a vast interconnected system — a sort of gigantic clockwork mechanism. But some incredibly fast movements, like the speed of light, did not quite fit the calculations. Neither did the movements of certain huge objects, like planets and stars. Albert Einstein (*see page 12*) led the way in devising a new scientific system, using more complex ideas such as relativity. At the same time, scientists were also delving inward to the world of atoms — the particles that atoms are made from and the forces that hold them together.

FAMOUS FIRSTS

HARNESSING WIND ENERGY

As long ago as A.D. 700, people in the Middle East were harnessing the power of the wind. Wind blew against angled sails and turned them around, providing movement to lift water into irrigation ditches and grind grain into flour. A modern wind farm has many wind **turbines** with accurately designed blades. These turn generators to make electricity.

Windmills for grinding grain were once quite common. But a major problem with wind power is that it is unreliable. It is not windy every day.

Modern electricity-generating wind farms produce no chemical or radioactive pollution.

CATCH THE WIND
You can make a simple fan-shaped windmill and even use it to measure the strength of the wind.

You need
Square sheet of thin cardboard or plastic, pencil, scissors, wire, long stick of wood.

1. On cardboard or plastic, draw the pattern below. Cut along the dotted lines, and make small holes at the five circles.

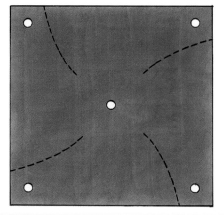

2. Fold the corners to the center. Push the wire through the corners and center hole.

3. Bend the wire over at the back, and loop it around the stick to secure the windmill in position. Check that it spins freely.

- Over the years, windmill design has improved. Now, the blades and top part, or cap, swivel around on a large, upright, central post. This means the blades can be swung around to face the wind when it blows in different directions.

Using the friction-reducing ideas on pages 20-21, can you think of ways to improve the windmill's design?

- Water mills have been used to operate machinery for over 2,500 years, and to grind grain for about 2,000 years.

- Some waterwheels are horizontal, lying at the surface of the water. Others are vertical. Those where the water flows under the wheel are called undershot waterwheels. Those where it flows onto the top of the wheel (like the model at right) are overshot waterwheels.

Vertical undershot waterwheel

CATCH THE WATER
This simple model waterwheel works as a "flow-measurer" to see which tap is most powerful.

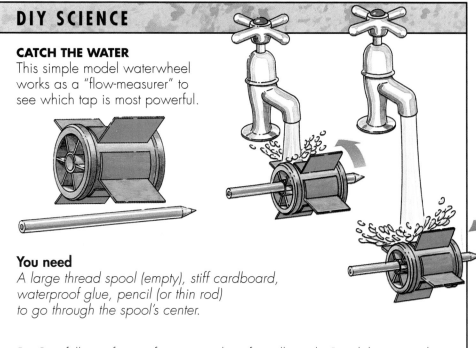

You need
A large thread spool (empty), stiff cardboard, waterproof glue, pencil (or thin rod) to go through the spool's center.

1. Carefully cut four or five rectangles of cardboard. Bend them at right angles. Glue one side of each to the spool, evenly spaced around it.

2. Put the spool on the pencil or rod, so it spins freely. Test your waterwheel under various taps at your home, including in the basement and outside. A short tap may not turn the waterwheel very fast.

3. Longer taps will probably spin the waterwheel much faster.

Gravity, one of the fundamental forces, holds rings of dust around the planet Saturn.

MOVEMENTS IN THE ATOM

The idea that all matter and substances are made of tiny particles was discussed by ancient Greek thinkers almost 2,500 years ago. The modern version of this theory became established during the early nineteenth century. The word *atom*, meaning uncuttable or indivisible, was used for these basic particles. But by the end of the nineteenth century, scientists realized that atoms could be cut up. Atoms were made of even smaller particles — electrons, protons, and neutrons. Two scientists who suggested ideas about atomic structure were New Zealand-born Ernest Rutherford (1871-1937) and Danish physicist Niels Bohr (1885-1962).

Shell-like orbit

Electrons

Nucleus

Rutherford suggested an atom was like a tiny solar system. Electrons whizzed around a central nucleus of protons and neutrons, like miniature planets around a sun. Bohr proposed that electrons went around the nucleus, but only at certain distances in layers or shells, as shown. Each shell holds a maximum number of electrons. This is the most popular view today.

Another batch of new ideas grew into physics, which says energy comes in tiny packets or units, called quanta. Quantum physics deals with these immensely small particles and brief events. Both relativity and quantum physics are important for the very small and the very large. However, for most everyday events here on Earth, we can still use the simpler mechanics and "clockwork universe" of Sir Isaac Newton.

FASCINATING FACTS

- Some of the doubts about atoms being indivisible came from studies of radioactivity. Other doubts came from the mysterious rays known as cathode rays, produced by a device shaped like a glass "dumbbell," known as a Crookes tube.

- It was finally discovered that cathode rays were streams of electrons. You probably use them every day — they are the particles that hit the inside of a television screen and cause it to glow.

FAMOUS FIRSTS

FOUR FUNDAMENTAL FORCES Today, most scientists believe that there are four basic or fundamental forces in the Universe *(see below)*. All other forces are versions or combinations of these. Three of the forces have the most effect at the incredibly tiny scale of particles of atoms. The fourth, gravitational force, is effective on the more everyday scale of plants and animals — and also on the scale of planets and stars.

The strong nuclear force holds together the smallest particles, quarks and electrons.

The weak nuclear force binds together the particles inside an atom's nucleus.

The electromagnetic force keeps electrons near the nucleus and holds atoms in molecules.

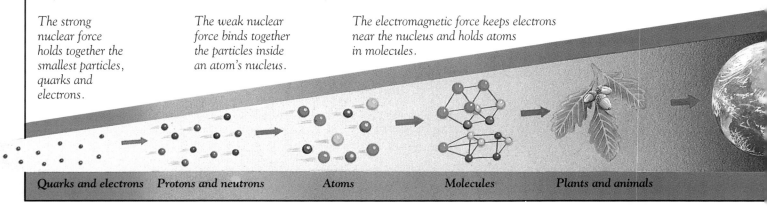

| Quarks and electrons | Protons and neutrons | Atoms | Molecules | Plants and animals |

FOREVER MOVING?

People through the ages have dreamed of making a machine or device that, once started, will move or work forever.

This is known as a perpetual motion machine. However, the laws of energy and motion tell us that this is impossible. Even with the best-designed bearings and the best lubricating oils, moving parts lose some of their kinetic energy as heat energy because of friction. With no energy coming in, the machine eventually stops.

One idea for perpetual motion is a sealed glass container housing plants and a few animals. The plants grow; the animals eat them. Their wastes, gases, and moisture are recycled in the soil. But plants only grow in the light (see page 11). So energy is entering the container, as light.

In this perpetual motion design, spheres contain the heavy metal known as mercury, which sloshes from one side to the other. The idea is to increase angular momentum (see page 19). But like all machines, it gradually slows down due to friction.

MAKE TASTY SALT

This simplified demonstration shows how atoms join together to make molecules.

You need

Apple, orange, cherries, toothpicks.

1. The apple represents an atom of sodium. It is dangerously active because it has a spare electron in its outer shell — the cherry.

2. The orange depicts an atom of chlorine, a poisonous gas. It has room for one more electron. Stick the cherry that is attached to the apple to the orange. Sodium's lone electron slots into chlorine's gap. The result is sodium chloride — table salt.

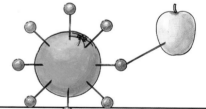

The gravitational force is weakest but acts over the longest distances, between stars and galaxies.

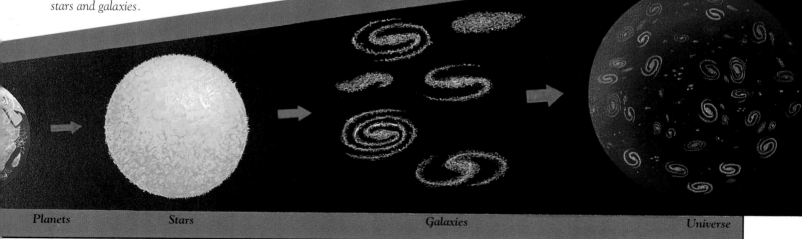

Planets   Stars   Galaxies   Universe

SIMPLE MACHINES

What is the connection between a corkscrew and a combine harvester; an egg whisk and a racing car? In each case, the first is a simple machine; the second is a more complex machine based on the simple machine. Simple machines include the **lever**, ramp, wedge, screw, roller, wheel and axle, and pulley. Complex machines are made of simple ones.

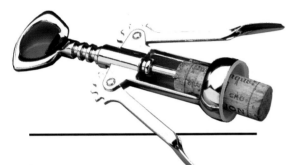

Imagine you are marooned all alone on an island. You have plenty of food and fresh water, but you have no shelter. So you build a log cabin. You need a sharp stone to make an ax to cut the wood. You also need a long pole to lever the logs into position. You may have to use smaller logs as rollers to move the bigger ones.

You have made and used three simple machines. These are the wedge, lever, and roller. A simple machine is a device that helps in some way. It does a job that the human body by itself could not do efficiently. Simple machines make a job or task easier.

A wedge is a double-version of what is perhaps the simplest of simple machines, the ramp. A ramp is a slope or incline, usually used for getting heavy things to a higher position. Ancient people used ramps to build their great structures, such as the pyramids.

SPECIAL FX

LIFT A FRIEND WITH A FINGER
A long lever lets you lift the weight of your friend with just one of your fingers.

You need
Long plank of wood, short log, friend, adult supervision.

1. With an adult to help you, place the log under the plank, near one end, as shown. Have a friend sit on the end of the plank nearest the log. Press with one finger at the other end.

2. Your friend should slowly rise in the air. If not, move the log nearer the friend. You use only a small force to move a large weight.

SIMPLY HUGE

The pyramids of ancient Egypt were built over four thousand years ago using simple machines such as levers and rollers. The Great Pyramid near Giza is the largest. Completed in about 2550 B.C., it was the tomb for Pharaoh Kheops. Each of the pyramid's four sides is 755 feet (230 meters) long. The pyramid was once almost 492 feet (150 m) tall, but its surface stone no longer exists.

The pyramids were constructed without using engines or motors. The builders had only a selection of simple machines and the power of the human body. Thousands of men did the work.

- Ancient Greek scientist and thinker Archimedes was supposed to have said: "Give me a lever long enough and a place to rest it, and I will move the world." In theory, he would be right. The problem is that the lever would be millions of miles (kilometers) long with nowhere in space for it to pivot.

- Devices such as bolt-cutters, tree pruners, and the bone-shears used by surgeons have very long handles and very short blades. This gives enough leverage for almost anyone to cut through a metal bolt, tough branch, or bone.

DIY SCIENCE

TYPES OF LEVERS

A basic lever consists of a rigid bar and a place where it can pivot, called the **fulcrum**. The force which does the moving is known as the effort. The object that is moved is the load. There are three main classes of levers. They differ in the positions of their fulcrum, effort, and load. Notice various levers — a wheelbarrow, scissors, or a door latch. Which class of lever is each of them? Some levers are less obvious, like the doorknob for pulling a door open. The handle is the place where you apply the effort. The fulcrum is the door hinge. The load is the weight of the door itself.

In the class-one lever, the fulcrum is in the middle, between the effort and load. In a pair of pliers, the fulcrum is the pivot joint, the effort is where you squeeze with your hand, and the load is what you grip in the pliers' jaws.

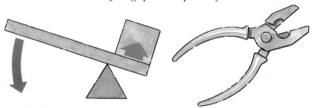

In the class-two lever, the load is in the middle, between the effort and fulcrum. In a pair of nutcrackers, the load is the nut, the effort is where you squeeze the handles, and the fulcrum is the pivot.

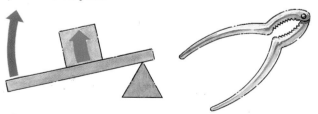

In the class-three lever, the effort is in the middle, between the fulcrum and load. In tongs, the effort is the middle part of the tong where you squeeze, the fulcrum is the bendable end, and the load is the object you are picking up.

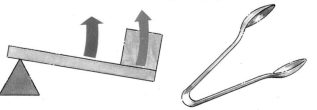

Pulling or rolling a stone up a ramp in small stages was easier than lifting it directly upward. But this example illustrates an important principle about simple machines. You do not get something for nothing. It may be easier to tow the stone block up a ramp. But you move the stone a much longer distance compared to lifting it straight up. Whichever method you use, the end result is that the total amount of work you do is the same.

This principle applies to most simple machines. They make the job easier, but there is always a drawback. For instance, you can lift a heavy weight by pressing down on a lever with your hands. You gain an advantage, called a mechanical advantage. This is the force you use compared to the force the lever can exert. So if you press on the lever with a force of about 1 pound (or 1 kilogram), and the lever produces a force of about 10 pounds (10 kilograms), the mechanical advantage is 1:10. But there is a corresponding disadvantage. The weight moves a small distance, while your hands must move a longer distance. Say your hands move about 100 inches (100 cm), but the weight moves only 10 inches (10 cm). To move the weight 100 inches (100 cm), you would have to move it in ten stages. In the end, you would have done ten sets of moving your 1-pound (1-kg) weight 100 inches (100 cm). The total work done is the same as if you had moved a 10-pound (10-kg) weight by 100 inches (100 cm) in one stage. But using the lever to divide the work into ten stages is easier!

FAMOUS FIRSTS

THE "LIQUID" LEVER

The hydraulic jack works like a lever. A small force moves a much bigger weight, but it moves farther than the weight. Hydraulic devices depend on Pascal's law as stated by French scientist Blaise Pascal (1623-1662). Press a liquid, and the force acts equally all through it. Imagine a small force pushing a small piston. This force is transmitted through the fluid to a piston ten times the size. The large piston can move a load ten times as big as the force, but moves it just one-tenth as far.

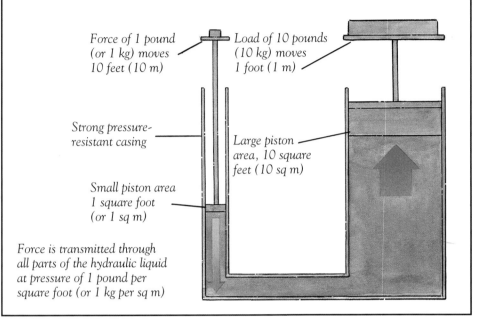

Force of 1 pound (or 1 kg) moves 10 feet (10 m)

Load of 10 pounds (10 kg) moves 1 foot (1 m)

Strong pressure-resistant casing

Large piston area, 10 square feet (10 sq m)

Small piston area 1 square foot (or 1 sq m)

Force is transmitted through all parts of the hydraulic liquid at pressure of 1 pound per square foot (or 1 kg per sq m)

FASCINATING FACTS

- An earth-moving machine has many hydraulic systems. The large diesel engine provides the power for the hydraulic pumps. The pumps transmit forces through the liquid in flexible pipes or hoses to the large pistons. The pistons move the digger arms with tremendous force, and these act as levers. As the piston fills with liquid, more liquid comes in through adjustable valves, so the system does not run out of "push."

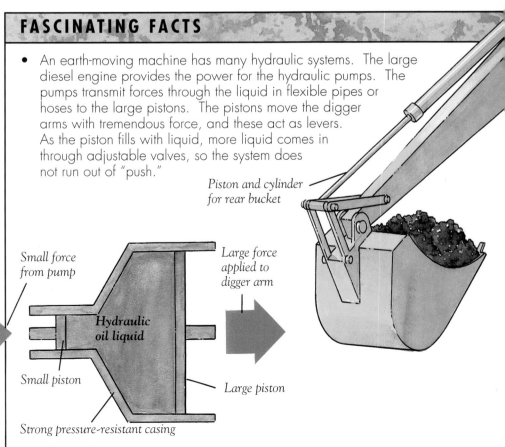

Piston and cylinder for rear bucket

Small force from pump

Large force applied to digger arm

Hydraulic oil liquid

Small piston

Large piston

Strong pressure-resistant casing

FAMOUS FIRSTS

THE GAS LAWS

Several scientists contributed to the study of gases — what happens when you squeeze, stretch, warm, or cool them. Boyle's Law is named after Irish-English chemist Robert Boyle (1627-1691). If a gas stays the same temperature, then as its volume goes down, its pressure goes up. Charles's law is named after French physicist Jacques Charles (1746-1823). If a gas stays the same pressure, its volume increases as its temperature goes up. These laws have many important uses, from calculating the flying abilities of aircraft to improving the design of car engines (see page 41).

DIY SCIENCE

WHY THE BIKE PUMP GETS WARM

When you inflate the tires on a bicycle, does the pump in your hands feel warm or even hot? This is due to the effect of pressure on gases, as described by the gas laws (above). As you push down on a gas, its molecules get closer together. They bounce and bang into each other and into the walls of the container — the pump — more often. These extra collisions have the effect of raising the temperature.

SPECIAL FX

THE PRESSURE ROCKET

You can place air under pressure, just like a liquid. But air is compressible, which means it gets pressed smaller. Using this rocket, show how air pressure (see page 32) can build up.

You need

Plastic bottle, cardboard, scissors, glue, cork with center hole, bicycle pump, short plastic tube, tape, water, adult supervision. Be extremely careful with this project.

1. Cut tail-fins from cardboard as shown, and glue them to the bottle. Tape the bicycle pump tube securely to the plastic tube. Carefully push the tube through the cork. Put some water in the bottle, push the cork into the neck, and turn it all upside-down, as shown.

2. Pump air into the bottle. As it is forced in, pressure builds up. Finally, the cork and compressed air come blasting out of the neck with a "pop." The rocket shoots into the air according to Newton's third law.

Piston and cylinder for second section of rear arm

The backhoe has a large, wide front bucket for bulldozing and lifting large items, and a small, narrow rear bucket on a longer arm, for reaching farther and digging narrow trenches.

Hydraulic hose

Piston and cylinder for front bucket

A hydraulic machine is like a "liquid" lever. You cannot compress (or squeeze smaller) liquids, such as oil or water. When you apply a force to them, the force is transmitted all through the liquid and presses on every part of the liquid's container. The force can also press on a piston and move it (*see page 28*). If a force is applied by a small piston, it can be transmitted through the liquid to a larger piston and turned into a bigger force. So a small force or effort can move a much bigger weight or load. But, like the lever, there is a disadvantage. The effort must move much farther than the load.

The wedge is two ramps placed back-to-back. It can be used for splitting or pushing objects apart, as in the stone ax you made on the island. Twist a long wedge into a corkscrew shape, and you have another useful, simple machine called the screw. This was supposedly invented by Archimedes of ancient Greece. He was an expert mathematician who devised many formulas in geometry. He carried out experiments — unusual in his day — and invented numerous machines, gadgets, and weapons.

In many bigger machines, screws are used to apply pressure. In science, the word *pressure* has a specific meaning. It is a measure of how much force there is in a certain area. So it is measured in two units, as force (weight) per area. The standard scientific unit of pressure is the pascal, named after French scientist and philosopher Blaise Pascal (*see page 28*).

FAMOUS FIRSTS

THE ARCHIMEDES SCREW

Archimedes (287-212 B.C.) was possibly the most famous scientist of ancient Greece. But it is not certain that he invented the screw that bears his name. Someone else may have thought of the idea first before Archimedes described it and developed its design in a more scientific way. The Archimedes screw is based on another simple machine, the wedge. A wedge in a corkscrew shape is a screw. As it turns, it can pull or push or twist substances past itself, or twist itself into a substance. The screw has thousands of uses in all types of machines.

Long ago, the Archimedes screw lifted water from a low pool or river up to irrigation ditches and channels in the fields. As the screw turned, it pushed water up its helical ramp.

Tube casing

Water in at low level

Central screw — a snug fit in the tube

DIY SCIENCE

HOW MANY SCREWS?

Simple machines based on the screw are common. The raised wedge-shaped part of a screw is called the thread. In wood screws, the thread's diameter gradually gets wider, so its shape is a combination of corkscrew and spiral. In a bolt, the screw thread has the same diameter its entire length. A wrench is used to turn the bolt head or nut. Look around your home and school to find screws that are being used for securing, pulling, pushing, and adjusting.

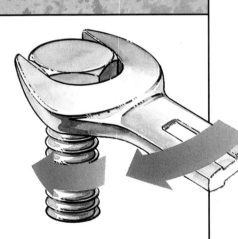

A screw has the same advantage and disadvantage as a lever. It converts a small force into a large one, as the wrench turns the bolt head. But the small force on the shaft of the wrench must move much farther than the large one at the bolt head.

The propeller of a plane is sometimes called an "air screw" because of the way it twists and screws through the air. The propeller of a ship is also known as a screw.

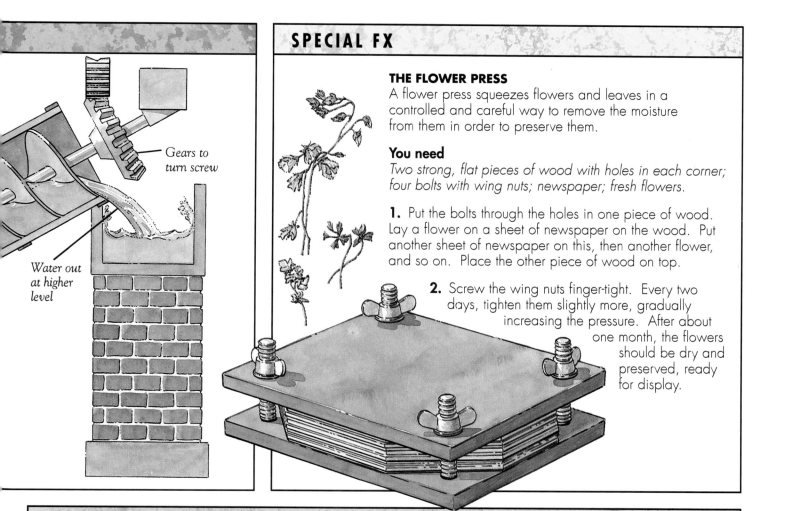

Gears to turn screw

Water out at higher level

THE FLOWER PRESS

A flower press squeezes flowers and leaves in a controlled and careful way to remove the moisture from them in order to preserve them.

You need

Two strong, flat pieces of wood with holes in each corner; four bolts with wing nuts; newspaper; fresh flowers.

1. Put the bolts through the holes in one piece of wood. Lay a flower on a sheet of newspaper on the wood. Put another sheet of newspaper on this, then another flower, and so on. Place the other piece of wood on top.

2. Screw the wing nuts finger-tight. Every two days, tighten them slightly more, gradually increasing the pressure. After about one month, the flowers should be dry and preserved, ready for display.

FASCINATING FACT

- Screws and screw-type devices are almost everywhere, even in very modern machines like the combine harvester. Inside the combine, some screws are longer than you are tall and shaped like wide-bladed corkscrews. They are called augers, and they move various parts of the crop around inside the combine. Another device that does a similar job is the conveyor belt.

The distribution auger pushes the separated grain up into the storage tank.

The main auger carries the freshly cut crop up inside the machine, ready to separate the grain from the unwanted parts.

At sea level, air presses on every square inch of your body with a weight of 14.7 pounds (or 1 kg per sq cm). You are born into this pressure, so you do not feel it at all.

Circular motion is a special form of movement (*see page 19*). It has its own simple machines. Wheels on their axles and rollers reduce the friction caused by dragging or scraping an object along the ground. Instead of a flat surface sliding along the ground, each part of the curved surface of a wheel comes down onto the ground. The wheel surface presses onto the ground, then lifts away again, with hardly any sideways movement. The friction of a wheel rotating on its axle, or an axle inside its hub, can be lessened by specially designed bearings and lubricating oils. Early bearings were made of leather or very hard, shiny wood. Today's ball bearings are made from extremely hard, shiny metals, such as special types of steel. A roller bearing, which uses short rods or rollers instead of balls, can stand much more pressure than a ball bearing but is not quite so friction-free. It is used for heavy-duty applications, such as in bull-dozers, tanks, and similar vehicles and machines.

There are many variations on the device called the crank. A basic crank is a straight part attached to a wheel, which rotates with the wheel around the same axle point. A familiar example is the straight part attached to a bicycle's pedal.

ROLLING ALONG

The great blocks of stone used in ancient wonders, such as Egyptian pyramids and Stonehenge in England, were often quarried many miles (km). They were probably pushed on rollers made of straight tree trunks. A roller is like a long wheel without an axle *(see pages 26-27)*.

Workers used long tree trunks to roll stone blocks over the ground.

Each tree trunk was taken from back to front as the stone block moved along.

DIY SCIENCE

PUSH A BRICK WITH A FINGER

You can recreate the scene above in miniature, to see how rollers help.

You need

A brick, pencils, a flat piece of wood (with natural finish, not varnished or polished).

Large force needed to overcome friction

1. Place the brick on the wood. Try to push it along with one finger. Is it difficult?

2. Place the pencils underneath. Feel how much easier it is to push the brick along with one finger.

Smaller force needed due to reduced friction

THE WHEEL

The wheel is another simple machine. It is a disk or circle that rotates around its center, usually on a rod called an axle. We do not know exactly who to thank for this amazingly useful invention. Well-made wheels are shown in paintings, mosaics, and sculptures of the Sumerian people from about five thousand years ago in ancient Mesopotamia (modern-day Iraq). The first wheels may actually date from well before this time.

The ancient Sumerians had war chariots with solid wheels made of wood.

- The first use of the wheel and axle may have been as a potter's wheel for turning clay.

- The first wheels were solid wooden disks. Spoked wheels were probably invented in northern Syria almost four thousand years ago. They were much lighter and easier to roll. They could bend and flex slightly for a smoother ride.

- The wheel spread throughout the various countries mainly by warfare and invasion. Soldiers with wheeled chariots pulled by horses could move faster and carry more weight than soldiers on foot.

- The wheel was used on children's toys in ancient North and South America. But it did not appear on wheeled vehicles there until the Europeans arrived.

The pennyfarthing of Europe in the 1870s traveled a long way with one turn of the pedals.

PEDAL POWER

To propel the first bicycles of about 1790, riders pushed off the ground with their feet. In 1839, the first bicycle with pedals appeared. Each pedal was connected by a rod to a crank to the back wheel. As the pedal moved, the crank rotated the wheel. In the French version called the velocipede (1852), the cranks were attached directly to the front wheel.

The longer a crank, the more turning force it can produce, as in a lever (see page 34). This type of drill is a long crank that turns the drill bit with great force.

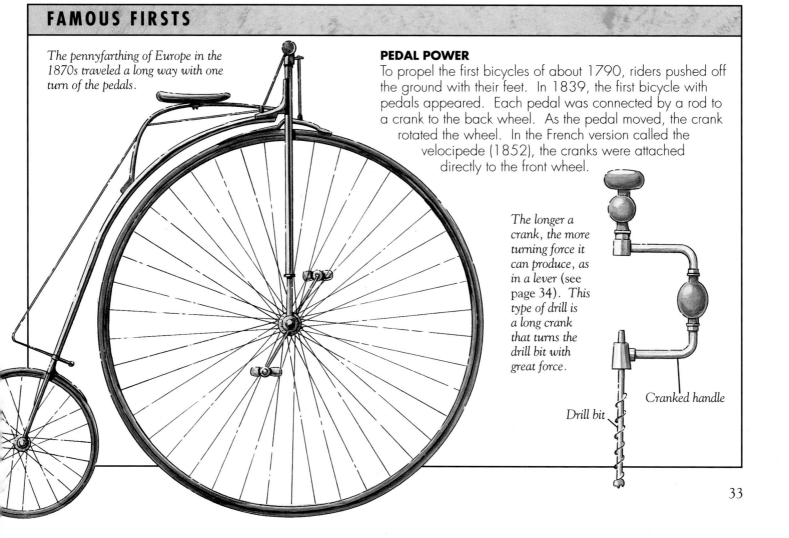

Cranked handle

Drill bit

33

It works like a "circular lever." The crank can turn the wheel with increased force. But it has the familiar drawback connected with mechanical advantage. The end of the crank has to move a longer distance.

There are also many variations on the pulley. A basic pulley is an axle bearing a wheel with a grooved or dished rim, into which fits string, rope, or cable. Linking pulleys together in a series produces another lever-type machine, called the pulley block, for lifting heavy weights with a smaller force. But the laws of simple machines still apply. To lift a weight about 3 feet (1 m) with a pulley block, you might have to pull through about 30 feet (10 m) of rope.

A further development of the rope and pulley is the chain and sprocket (toothed gear wheel). Several sprockets can be arranged into a gear system, as seen on a bicycle. In top gear, one turn of the pedals can make the back wheel turn twenty times. But the force needed to push the pedals around is correspondingly greater. So high gears are used mainly for going downhill when Earth's gravity also helps. In the lowest gear, one turn of the pedals makes the back wheel turn only once or even less. The force needed to push the pedals around is small. But the bike moves forward only a short distance. This is suitable for cycling up steep hills. But low gear soon tires the bicyclist on flat ground.

Bicycle gears are designed to let the bicyclist pedal at her or his own speed and amount of power all the time, whatever the

DIY SCIENCE

ANCHORS AWEIGH
The pulley-like machine once used on ships to haul up the heavy anchor was a **capstan**.

You need
An empty thread spool, a nail, a flat piece of wood, a pencil, tape, string, a weight, adult supervision.

Carefully nail the spool to the wood. Tie one end of the string to the spool. Tape the pencil firmly to the top of the spool. Tie the weight to the other end of the string.

In this model capstan, turn the pencil, which is the crank. See how the weight rises with little turning effort.

On a real capstan from long ago, poles fit into the central drum. These were removed afterward to give more space to the cramped ship.

Largest sprocket

Derailleur gear-change mechanism

Derailleur sprockets pull chain sideways to change gear

SPECIAL FX

PULLEYS AND GEARS

Pulleys or gears convert a small force into a large one, but with the usual disadvantage that the small force moves farther than the large one. The system of pulleys for lifting, shown here, does this.

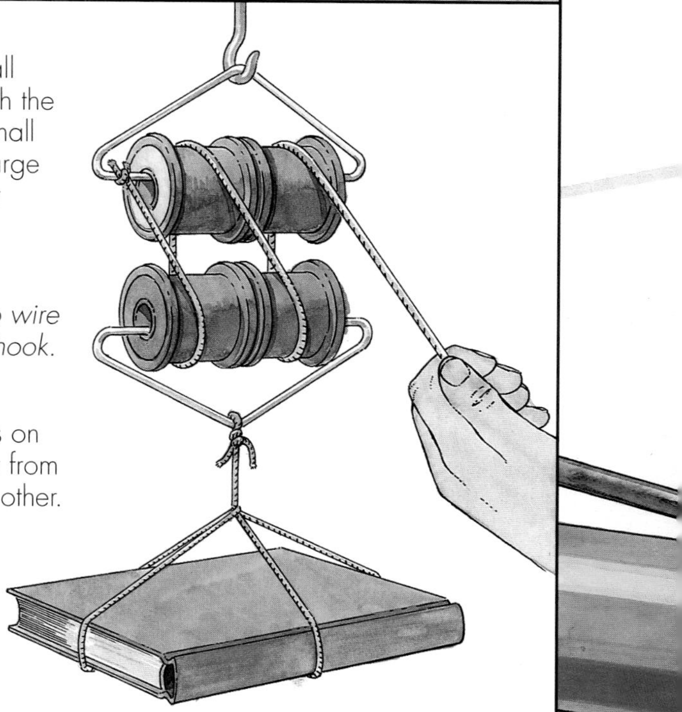

You need
Four empty thread spools, two wire coat hangers, string, weight, hook.

1. Undo the coat hangers as shown, and thread two spools on each. Hang one coat hanger from the hook. Tie a weight to the other. Tie and loop the string on the spools, as shown.

2. Pull the end of the string. The weight rises easily, compared to lifting it directly. But notice how far you must pull the string to raise the book only a short way.

3. Try different pulley systems, using only one spool on each coat hanger. Or perhaps put three or even four spools on each hanger. Thread the string around them using the same basic pattern, as shown above. Notice how more pulleys make it easier to lift the weight — but you have to pull more and more string to move the weight the same distance.

This egg whisk has a large sprocket with many teeth that turn small sprockets. One turn of the handle makes the whisks turn many times, but with correspondingly less force.

FAMOUS FIRSTS

BICYCLE GEARS
Derailleur gears were developed in 1899. With the chain on the smallest rear sprocket, one turn of the pedals turns the rear wheel several times. With the chain on the largest rear sprocket, one turn of the pedals turns the rear wheel far fewer times.

Derailleur frame

Chain

FASCINATING FACTS

- Using very high gears, special speed bicycles can go faster than many cars. The world record for a bicycle is 152 miles (245 km) per hour. But this was achieved with the aid of another vehicle traveling just in front of the bicycle. The vehicle had a large, curved windshield to cut down the air resistance reaching the bicycle.

- Using multi-pulley systems, large cranes can lift hundreds of tons. The world's most powerful lifter is a floating crane with two hoists, each capable of raising 7,715 tons (7,000 metric tons).

terrain. The cyclist changes the gears for going uphill, downhill, and along level ground. The cyclist's speed changes — but his or her legs and feet always keep the pedals turning at the same rate. Cars and trucks also have gears for a similar reason. When a car engine turns very slowly, it does not have very much turning force, or torque. Its torque is much larger when it is turning at medium or high rate. So in a car, if you try to start off in top gear, the engine does not have enough torque to get the car moving. It shudders and stalls. If you start off in first gear, the engine speeds up at once and has enough torque to set the car in motion easily. Like the gears on a bicycle, the gears in a car allow the engine to turn at its most comfortable and powerful rate, no matter what the speed of the car. However, as with pulleys, levers, screws, and other simple machines, you do not get something for nothing. Newton's laws apply, and energy cannot be created or destroyed — only conserved or converted in form.

Fulcrum

Load transmitted along brake cable

The brake handle is a class-one lever. Your fingers apply the effort. The pull is transmitted along the brake cable to press the brake blocks against the wheel rim.

The wheel and tire reduce friction because of their circular shape. The tire comes into contact with the ground, then lifts away again without scraping or dragging. Air pressure is transmitted equally all around the tire according to Pascal's law.

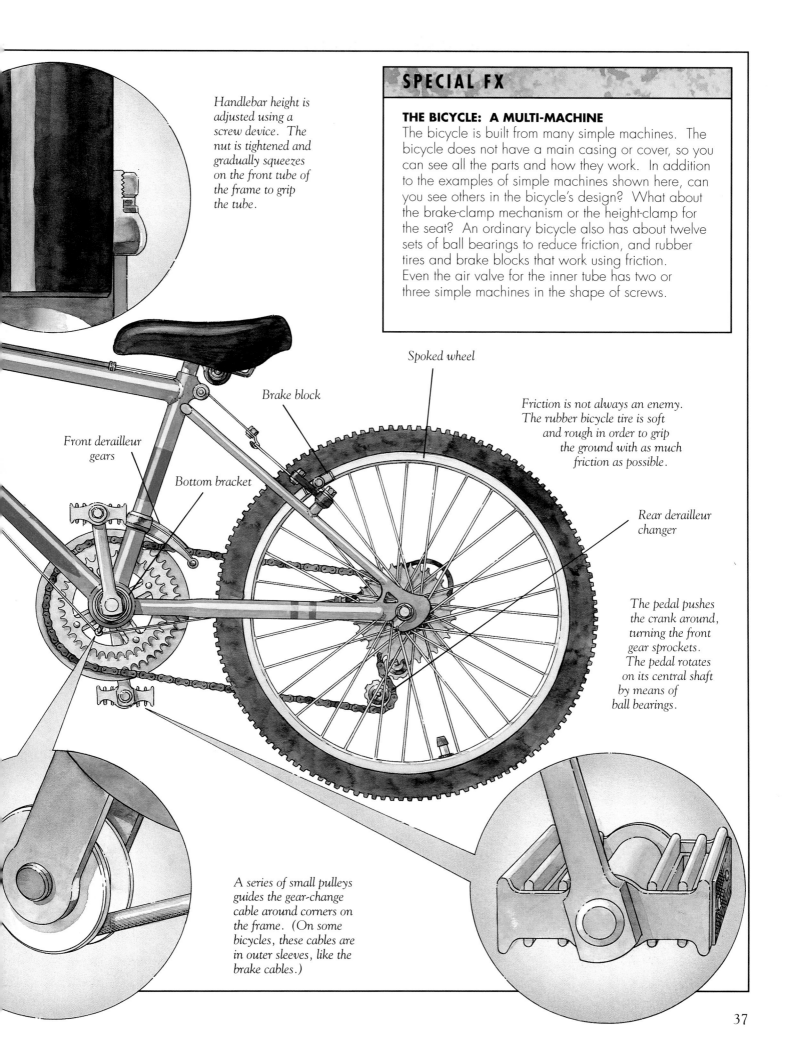

Handlebar height is adjusted using a screw device. The nut is tightened and gradually squeezes on the front tube of the frame to grip the tube.

THE BICYCLE: A MULTI-MACHINE
The bicycle is built from many simple machines. The bicycle does not have a main casing or cover, so you can see all the parts and how they work. In addition to the examples of simple machines shown here, can you see others in the bicycle's design? What about the brake-clamp mechanism or the height-clamp for the seat? An ordinary bicycle also has about twelve sets of ball bearings to reduce friction, and rubber tires and brake blocks that work using friction. Even the air valve for the inner tube has two or three simple machines in the shape of screws.

Spoked wheel

Brake block

Friction is not always an enemy. The rubber bicycle tire is soft and rough in order to grip the ground with as much friction as possible.

Front derailleur gears

Bottom bracket

Rear derailleur changer

The pedal pushes the crank around, turning the front gear sprockets. The pedal rotates on its central shaft by means of ball bearings.

A series of small pulleys guides the gear-change cable around corners on the frame. (On some bicycles, these cables are in outer sleeves, like the brake cables.)

ENGINES

The Egyptian pyramids were built using the muscle power of millions of men. But the world has changed. To carry out huge tasks, such as building a large structure or transporting goods and people, today we use machines powered by engines. An engine uses the energy in its fuel to do the job.

Our world is full of engines. They give us the power to do large jobs and to do them faster than we could using just our bodies alone. People have harnessed natural power, such as wind and flowing water, for thousands of years. But these sources of energy are limited to certain places and certain times. An engine can be built or taken anywhere, provided it can be supplied with fuel.

Steam engines were the first common types of engines. They were originally developed to pump out water that seeped into mines. As the Industrial Revolution of the eighteenth and nineteenth centuries grew, steam engines were installed in factories and put on wheels to make locomotives.

The steam engine is what is known as an external combustion engine. Its fuel, usually wood or coal, combusts (burns) outside the engine. The combustion heats water into steam. This is important because steam takes up 1,600 times more space than the amount of water it came from. So water changed into steam produces tremendous pressure, which can be used to push pistons and turn cranks.

FAMOUS FIRSTS

STEAM ON THE RIGHT LINES
The world's first steam-powered public railway was the Stockton & Darlington Railway in England. It opened in September of 1825. Its steam locomotive was the *Locomotion* designed by George Stephenson (1781-1848). The *Locomotion* weighed 7.7 tons (7 metric tons) and could pull a load of 55 tons (50 metric tons) at a speed of 15 miles (24 km) per hour. George and his son Robert then improved the steam locomotive and called it the *Rocket (right)*. It won a competition in 1829 for the best locomotive and was chosen for the Liverpool & Manchester Railway Company in England.

High-pressure steam hauls a train weighing over 11,000 tons (10,000 metric tons).

Wooden and metal frame

The pioneer steam locomotive Rocket won a speed competition called the Rainhill Trials in 1829. It could travel at 29 miles (47 km) per hour — an astonishing speed for the time. Some people thought that with its glowing fire and belching smoke, it was the work of the devil.

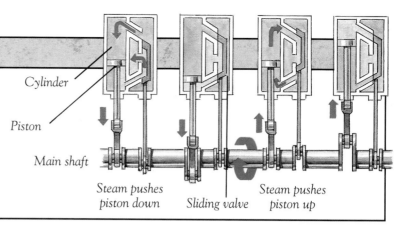

GETTING MORE POWER

The double-acting steam engine can produce more power than normally from the same amount of steam. It is more efficient — a vitally important feature for any engine. A sliding valve next to the piston switches the flow of steam from one side of the piston to the other. The valve is operated by a connecting rod linked to the main shaft.

Cylinder

Piston

Main shaft

Steam pushes piston down

Sliding valve

Steam pushes piston up

— *Smokestack*

Steam regulator

Water was heated and turned to high-pressure steam in the many tubes inside the boiler. The entire boiler was enclosed in an outer cylindrical casing. The multi-tube boiler design quickly became standard. The steam traveled along pipes to the cylinders.

High-pressure steam spurted into the cylinder and pushed the piston along. As this happened on one side of the locomotive, the steam in the piston on the other side was let out through a valve, and the wheel pushed the piston back in.

Non-driven wheel

The piston pushed a connecting rod joined to the wheel crank. Like the pedal on a bicycle, this turned the wheel around. The Rocket *had two large drive-wheels at the front. Later locomotives had four or even six, usually near the back.*

FAMOUS FIRSTS

THE STEAM TURBINE

A **turbine** *(see page 42)* is a machine with angled fan-like blades that spins around. During the 1870s in the early days of electricity generation, steam engines with pistons and cylinders were used to turn generators. But they were not very efficient. By 1884, Irish-born engineer Charles Parsons (1854-1931) had developed a practical steam turbine. Steam rushed past the angled blades and spun the central shaft, which was linked to the generator. The steam turbine was a tremendous success and is still used in power stations today.

SPECIAL FX

CLEAN WITH STEAM

Steam-cleaning machines remove dirt, grit, and oil from various engines and vehicles. An intense, super hot, super-pressurized jet of steam shoots from a long, wand-like tube called a lance. It blasts away the dirt. Special soap additives in the steam help to dissolve grease and oil.

FASCINATING FACTS

- In 1698, Thomas Savery designed a steam engine to pump floodwater from mines. In 1712, Thomas Newcomen made a more efficient version, as did James Watt in 1788. In 1804, Richard Trevithick put a steam engine on wheels to make the first locomotive to haul rocks and coal in mines.

- Steam power required fuel — wood or coal. Coal mines soon covered the landscape in some areas long ago.

FAMOUS FIRSTS

CARS AND MOTORBIKES

Self-propelled vehicles, called automobiles, have been around since about 1770. The first designs were powered by steam engines, but they were dirty, noisy, and not very efficient or suitable for passengers. The first successful wheeled vehicle with an internal combustion (gasoline) engine was a two-wheeler designed and built by Gottlieb Daimler in 1885. This vehicle, *Einspur*, was the first motorcycle. The first automobile was a three-wheeler with a single cylinder engine called the Motorwagen. It was tested in late 1885 by its designer-builder, Karl Benz.

The first car to be made in large quantities was Karl Benz's Viktoria in 1890.

The exhaust pipes guide used air away from the engine. A good exhaust design reduces the overall engine noise. In addition, it makes sure the burned fuel-air mixture can leave the cylinder as quickly as possible.

The cylinder head contains the piston. The head has many flat flanges called fins on it. These give off as much excess heat as possible from the combustions inside the cylinder into the surrounding air.

The next advance was the internal combustion engine developed during the mid-to-late 1800s. In this type of engine, the fuel and air mixture combusts, or burns, inside the engine in the cylinder. As in the steam engine, the gases resulting from the combustion take up far more space than the original fuel-air mixture, and this provides the power to push the piston along. Most internal combustion engines use either gasoline or diesel fuel.

The motorcycle's chain drive and sprockets are similar to those on a bicycle, but stronger and heavier, to take the extra strain.

The gears are housed in the transmission, which is just below and behind the engine.

SPECIAL FX

MIXING FUEL AND AIR

The carburetor is the part of a vehicle that mixes gasoline and air in precisely the right amounts so they will combust inside the cylinder. There are several designs of carburetors. In this version, the fuel flows from the main fuel tank into a small reservoir, the float chamber. It goes along a pipe and squirts from a tiny nozzle-hole, spraying into the air that is flowing to the cylinder.

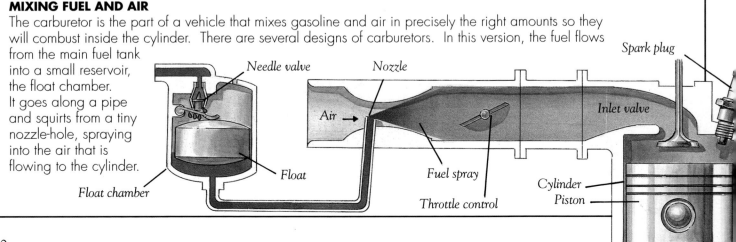

Needle valve

Nozzle

Spark plug

Air →

Inlet valve

Float

Fuel spray

Cylinder

Float chamber

Throttle control

Piston

- Gasoline and diesel fuels are made from oil (petroleum). In some areas, the countryside above oil reserves is dotted with pumps drawing oil from the ground.

The motorcycle's heaviest part is the engine. This is positioned between the wheels and near the ground to keep the main weight low, for the best stability.

DIY SCIENCE

THE BALLOON INFLATER
A valve controls the flow of liquid or gas. It may stop the flow, switch it from one pipe to another, or allow only one-way movement.

You need
Strong cardboard, strong plastic, stapler, funnel, tape, glue, scissors, petroleum jelly, adult supervision.

1. Roll up cardboard into a tube just big enough to fit your funnel and tape it firmly.

2. Carefully cut a cardboard disk slightly larger than the tube. Cut slits around the edge and a hole in the center. Fold over the edges of the cardboard to make an end piece for the tube.

3. Staple a small plastic disk over the hole in the cardboard. Smear petroleum jelly between the disk and the cardboard to make an airtight seal.

4. Fit the end piece onto the cardboard tube, disk facing in. Glue and tape the end piece to form an airtight seal. Glue and tape the plastic funnel to the tube at the same end.

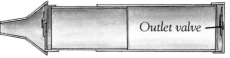

Inlet valve

Outlet valve

5. Roll another cardboard tube that just fits around the first one. Make another end piece as in steps 2 and 3, and attach it to the second tube, disk facing in. Put the tubes together.

6. Push a balloon over the funnel's spout. Pull — and air enters the pump. Push — and air enters the balloon.

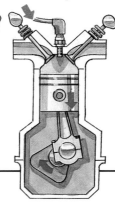

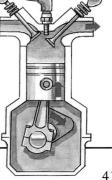

SPECIAL FX

THE FOUR-STROKE CYCLE
Most car engines run on a four-stroke cycle. This means the piston moves up, down, up and down again, for one complete working cycle. During each stroke, valves open and close as the fuel and air inside the cylinder changes. The valves are operated by rods or chains from the main shaft below the pistons. This is called the crankshaft because it has cranks *(see pages 32-34)* built into it.

Induction stroke
Fuel-air mixture is drawn in.

Compression stroke
Fuel-air mixture is squeezed by the piston.

Power stroke
Spark plug ignites fuel-air mixture, which explodes.

Exhaust stroke
Used fuel-air mixture is blown away.

FASCINATING FACTS

- The cost of building a rocket and sending it into space is enormous. In the end, most rocket parts float into space or burn up as they re-enter Earth's atmosphere.

- A space shuttle can be used many times. It consists of the orbiter craft, two rocket boosters, and a 770-ton (700-metric-ton) fuel tank.

- The rocket boosters help the orbiter's three main engines lift the craft to a great height. The boosters and tank fall back to Earth and are used again. The orbiter goes into space. It swoops back to Earth, landing like the world's biggest glider.

- The first rockets used gunpowder and bombarded enemies in twelfth-century Chinese wars.

- Modern rocket flight began in 1926 with the launch of the first liquid-fuel rocket, designed by American scientist Robert Goddard (1882-1945).

- The first rocket to launch a space satellite was the Soviet A, which put the satellite *Sputnik* into space in 1957.

Fuel in liquid form

Oxidizer in liquid form

Rocket engine (combustion chamber)

Around the turn of the century, engineers were making automobiles powered by steam or internal combustion, or even electricity as electric motors made their appearance. The internal combustion engine was the most convenient and so won the battle to power the car.

Today, rocket engines are designed to fly very high into outer space, where there is no oxygen. But oxygen is needed to power rocket engines. So rockets take not only fuel but also their own oxygen supply (as a liquid chemical called oxidizer) with them into outer space.

The jet engine was developed during the 1930s, mainly for use in aircraft. Today, it is the most familiar engine on large passenger aircraft and military planes of many kinds. Jets have allowed people to fly to the other side of the planet in a matter of hours. But like all engines, jet engines need energy from fuel, and fuel is a limited resource on Earth.

The BAe 125 is typical of today's relatively quiet, efficient jet planes. Weight for weight, the jet engine produces more power than any other type of engine.

Main engine casing

Exhaust

In the compressor, air is compressed or squeezed to tremendous pressure before being mixed with fuel. This pressurizing is done in several stages by different-shaped sets of compressor turbines.

Rear turbines

Jet fuel flows along pipes and is sprayed into the compressed air in the combustion chamber. The chamber is lined with special materials that resist the tremendous temperature. The fuel-air mixture catches fire in a continuous, controlled, roaring explosion.

Combustion chamber

Compressor turbines

As the hot gases roar from the combustion chamber, they spin another set of turbine blades. These are connected to the fan and compressor turbines by a long shaft that runs along the center of the engine, and provide the power to turn them.

THE JET AGE
The first jet engines were developed during the late 1930s in England and Germany. Part of the reason for the development was the demands of a possible war. The race to get ahead of the enemy with bigger, better, faster, and more powerful fighting machines is often the driving force behind progress in science, technology, and engineering. Both sides in World War II wanted to produce jet-engine fighter planes, which would be much faster than the propeller-driven ones.

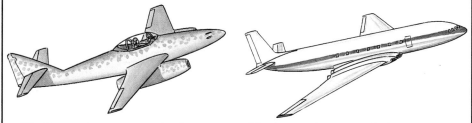

The first jet plane to go into battle was the German Messerschmitt Me 262 in 1944. However, it was too late to influence the war.

The first jet plane to regularly carry passengers was the British De Havilland Comet in 1952.

There are several main designs for jet engines. Pictured is the turbofan design, which is used for most modern passenger jet craft. It is named for the enormous turbine, or fan, at the front. The turbofan is very efficient and quiet.

Bypass ducting

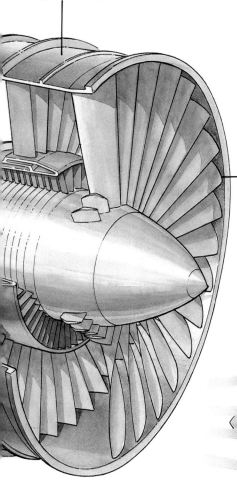

The blades of the main fan may be about 6.5 feet (2 m) long. They are made of titanium and other metals that are light and strong. The fan draws air into the main engine and also blows it through the bypass ducts, thereby acting partly as a propeller.

— Turbofan

The large front fan blows air both into and around the main engine. The outer or bypass airflow helps give extra thrust, and it also cools and quiets the main engine.

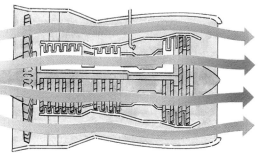

PROPULSION POWER
There are three main kinds of aircraft with engines. These are planes with jet engines; planes with propellers, usually driven by an internal combustion engine; and helicopters with whirling rotors, which have gas-turbine engines. Each flies differently.

In the jet engine, hot gases blast from the rear. According to Newton's third law of motion, this is the action, and the reaction is the plane being thrust forward.

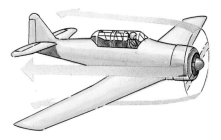

The propeller, or air screw (see page 30), consists of blades on a hub mounted on an engine-driven shaft. The rotating blades produce a forward thrust.

Helicopter rotors (blades) are long, thin wings that whirl around, lifting the craft. They also tilt slightly to make the helicopter go forward, sideways, or backward.

SAVING ENERGY

Every time you travel in a car, or purchase manufactured products, or even switch on a light, you are using energy. In most cases, this energy was once in the form of fossil fuels — coal, oil, and gas. We are using these precious forms of energy very quickly, and they are limited here on Earth. More than ever, we need to **conserve** energy and use forms of energy that are **renewable** — such as solar, wind, water, and tidal power.

DIY SCIENCE

THE ENERGY-EFFICIENT HOME

Look around your home or school to see how you can save energy. There are more and more new energy-saving ideas and gadgets. Compact fluorescent light bulbs may seem expensive at first. But they last for years and use less electricity than other bulbs. When you consider the savings in replacement bulbs and lower electric bills, compact fluorescents soon pay for themselves. In a typical house, most heat is lost through the roof, windows, and doors. But even solid brick walls let through heat, which represents lost energy. What are ways to insulate a home?

The first successful ship with an engine was the Clermont, *designed by Robert Fulton. Its steam engine powered the paddlewheels. It made regular trips along the Hudson River out of New York between 1807 and 1814.*

FASCINATING FACTS

- Deep in the ocean, on the seabed, is the only life in our world that does not depend on the Sun for energy. Hot gases containing energy-rich chemicals bubble up from deep in the Earth through cracks and holes in the seafloor, known as sulfur vents. Bacteria and other microbes feed on the

ENERGY AND TRANSPORTATION

Certain types of transportation — cars, planes, ships — have engines that use massive amounts of fuel. Perhaps you are able to walk to school, the store, the park, or the movies. But people are used to taking a form of transportation. The next time you are going a short distance, try walking, bicycling, sharing a car, or using public transportation. These all save energy.

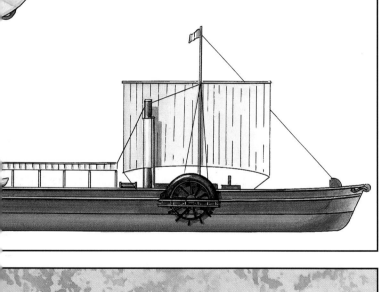

The first successful aircraft with an engine was the Flyer, *built by Wilbur and Orville Wright. It made the first powered plane flight in 1903 at Kitty Hawk, North Carolina.*

HOW MUCH ENERGY?

Around the world, the standard unit for measuring energy is the joule. Even when you are asleep, your body is using around four thousand joules each minute just to stay alive. The number of joules used by large machines and vehicles is huge. Most of this energy comes from fossil fuels, which cannot be replaced.

40 septillion joules
Energy given out by Sun per second

5 quadrillion joules
Energy used on Earth per hour

3 trillion joules
Energy in electricity from power station per hour

5 billion joules
Energy to make a tanker go about 2/3 mile (1 km)

315,000 joules
Energy to make a car run at 50 miles (80 km) per hour for seven seconds

Cooking in a microwave oven can be measured in hundreds of thousands of joules

200 joules
Energy for person to stand up

This diagram gives some idea of the approximate amounts of energy used for a variety of processes. It also reminds us that energy comes in many forms, from light and heat to chemicals and electricity.

energy in the chemicals. Small animals feed on the bacteria, and larger creatures feed on the small ones. There are crabs bigger than your hand, and worms longer than your body clustered in the endless darkness, in the fascinating community surrounding the sulfur vents.

GLOSSARY

atom — the smallest part of an element that can exist by itself or in combination with other atoms.

capstan — a pulley-like machine made of a vertical drum that can be rotated, and around which a cable is turned. Capstans move or raise weight.

chemical energy — the energy that is used to make a chemical substance. The energy is released when the substance is broken down.

conserve — to use carefully so as not to waste or completely use up.

ellipse — a closed curve that is shaped like an egg or oval.

friction — the moving or rubbing of one surface on another surface.

fulcrum — the point on which a lever turns or is supported when it is moving or lifting an object.

gravity — the force in nature that causes smaller objects to move toward the center of a heavenly body, such as Earth or other planets.

gyroscope — a scientific instrument with a mounted wheel that spins rapidly on an axis.

inertia — the tendency of an object to keep doing what it has been doing, either moving or staying still, until a force acts on it and changes the situation.

kinetic energy — the force possessed by an object as it moves.

lever (n) — a simple machine used for lifting weight; (v) to lift weight with the device.

molecule — the basic particle into which a substance can be divided and still be the same substance.

momentum — the force that an object possesses when it is in motion.

nuclear reaction — a response where nuclei, the central parts of atoms, break down into slightly lighter particles. This difference in weight becomes massive quantities of heat energy.

oscillation — a back-and-forth motion that moves from one extreme limit to the other.

pendulum — a weight that is hung so that it swings back and forth.

photosynthesis — a process in which plants use energy from the Sun to make food.

potential energy — the force an object possesses because of its position or condition. Potential energy is stored, waiting to be released.

renewable — having the ability to be restored or made new again.

spectrum — the various colors that are seen when light is broken up by a prism.

Stone Age — a prehistoric period of time when humans first used stone tools.

turbine — a device in which power is provided to turn the blades or vanes of a rotating wheel.

WEB SITES

www.energy.ca.gov/education/

www.pbs.org/tal/racecars/

www.wam.umd.edu/~tfagan/enrgyenv.html

tqd.advanced.org/3684/

www.windows.umich.edu/photoscience.la.asu.edu/photosyn/study.html

BOOKS

Alternative Energy (series). Houghton and Rickard (Gareth Stevens)

Ask Isaac Asimov (series). *How Do Airplanes Fly?* Isaac Asimov (Gareth Stevens)

Atoms: Building Blocks of Matter. T. Biel (Lucent)

Atoms and Molecules. P. Roxbee-Cox (EDC)

Cars: An Environmental Challenge. Wallace B. Black and Terri Willis (Childrens)

Cars, Bikes, Trains, and Other Land Machines. Ian Graham (Kingfisher)

Energy Alternatives. Barbara Keeler (Lucent)

Energy and Power. R. Spurgeon (EDC)

Energy Resources: Towards a Renewable Future. D. J. Herda and Margaret L. Madden (Watts)

Force: The Power Behind Movement. Eric Laithwarte (Watts)

Galileo. Leonard E. Fisher (Childrens)

Hands on Science (series). (Gareth Stevens)

Kids Can! (series). *The Kids' Science Book.* Robert Hirschfeld (Gareth Stevens)

Machines. C. Gifford (EDC)

Machines and How They Work. David Burnie (DK Publishing)

Record Breakers (series). *Machines and Inventions.* Peter Lafferty (Gareth Stevens)

Simple Science Projects (series). *Projects with Machines.* John Williams (Gareth Stevens)

Sir Isaac Newton. Hitzeroth and Leon (Lucent)

Solar Energy. Graham Rickard (Gareth Stevens)

Steam Engine. Beatrice Siegel (Walker and Co.)

The Sun. Isaac Asimov (Gareth Stevens)

Toy Box Science (series). (Gareth Stevens)

The Wheel and How It Changed the World. Ian Locke (Facts on File)

VIDEOS

Alternative Energies. (Film Ideas)

A Better Way to Go. (National Audiovisual)

Coal to Kilowatts. (AIMS Media)

The Energy Alternative Series: A Global Perspective. (RMI Media)

The Energy Series. (Barr Films)

Energy: What Now? (Pyramid Films)

Learning about Solar Energy. (AIMS Media)

The Sun. (Gareth Stevens)

PLACES TO VISIT

The Smithsonian Institution
1000 Jefferson Drive SW
Washington, D.C. 20560

Royal British Columbia Museum
675 Belleville Street
Victoria, British Columbia V8V 1X4

Science Place
1318 Second Avenue
Dallas, TX 75210

The Exploratorium
3601 Lyon Street
San Francisco, CA 94123

INDEX